Spelling Half Termly Tests

Year 4/P5

Clare Dowdall

William Collins' dream of knowledge for all began with the publication of his first book in 1819.
A self-educated mill worker, he not only enriched millions of lives, but also founded a flourishing
publishing house. Today, staying true to this spirit, Collins books are packed with inspiration,
innovation and practical expertise. They place you at the centre of a world of possibility
and give you exactly what you need to explore it.

Collins. Freedom to teach.

Collins
An imprint of HarperCollins*Publishers*
The News Building
1 London Bridge Street
London
SE1 9GF

Browse the complete Collins catalogue at **www.collins.co.uk**

© HarperCollins*Publishers* Limited 2018

10 9 8 7 6 5 4 3 2 1

ISBN 978-0-00-831153-7

All rights reserved. No part of this publication may be reproduced, stored in a retrieval system,
or transmitted in any form by any means, electronic, mechanical, photocopying, recording or otherwise,
without the prior written permission of the Publisher or a licence permitting restricted copying in
the United Kingdom issued by the Copyright Licensing Agency Ltd., Barnard's Inn, 86 Fetter Lane, London, EC4A 1EN.

British Library Cataloguing in Publication Data. A catalogue record for this publication is available from the British Library.

Author: Clare Dowdall
Publisher: Katie Sergeant
Senior Editor: Mike Appleton
Copyeditor: Tanya Solomons
Proofreader: Catherine Dakin
Cover designer: The Big Mountain Design, Ken Vail Graphic Design
Production controller: Katharine Willard

Contents

How to use this book — 4

Year 4/P5 Word Lists

Autumn Half Term 1 — 6
Autumn Half Term 2 — 8
Spring Half Term 1 — 10
Spring Half Term 2 — 12
Summer Half Term 1 — 14
Summer Half Term 2 — 16

Year 4/P5 Half Termly Tests

Autumn Half Term 1 Test A — 18
Autumn Half Term 1 Test B — 22
Autumn Half Term 2 Test A — 26
Autumn Half Term 2 Test B — 30
Spring Half Term 1 Test A — 34
Spring Half Term 1 Test B — 38
Spring Half Term 2 Test A — 42
Spring Half Term 2 Test B — 46
Summer Half Term 1 Test A — 50
Summer Half Term 1 Test B — 54
Summer Half Term 2 Test A — 58
Summer Half Term 2 Test B — 62

Answers

Answers in Context — 66
Word-only Answers — 90

Year 4/P5 Spelling Record Sheet — 92

How to use this book

Introduction

Collins Assessment Spelling Half Termly Tests have been designed to give you a consistent whole school approach to teaching and assessing spelling. Each photocopiable book covers the required rules, words and common exception words from the English National Curriculum statutory guidance and Spelling Appendix. For teachers in Scotland, the books can offer guidance and structure that is not provided in the Curriculum for Excellence Experiences and Outcomes or Benchmarks.

Revision of previous years' work is also included, where appropriate, to ensure children are building their skills to become confident and secure spellers. As standalone tests, independent of any teaching and learning scheme, *Collins Assessment Spelling Half Termly Tests* provide a structured way to assess progress in spelling, to identify areas for development, and to provide evidence towards expectations for each year group.

Why spelling matters

Spelling is a key focus of the 2014 English National Curriculum statutory requirements for writing, and the expectations and demands are significant. Out of a possible 70 marks, 20 are awarded for spelling in the Key Stage 2 National Tests, and 20 per cent of the new English Language GCSE 9–1 marks are allocated to spelling, punctuation and grammar. In Year 2, there is an optional Key Stage 1 English grammar, punctuation and spelling test that schools can use to help them make an assessment about children's spelling knowledge, as well as looking at their writing. In Scotland, the P1 literacy, P4 writing and P7 writing Scottish National Standardised Assessments assess spelling at early, first and second levels, respectively.

Focusing on spelling knowledge and skills will also benefit children's wider writing and will have a lasting impact across their education in primary, secondary and beyond. The *Collins Assessment Spelling Half Termly Tests* aim to support teachers to make assessments about children's confidence and use of required spelling rules and strategies, in order to support preparation for these standard assessment points.

How to use this book

The book is divided into two main sections. In the first section, between 30 and 36 weekly word lists are provided (depending on the year group). Each list contains six to ten words per half term. These words can be used for weekly tests and used in the classroom, or sent home with the children. They generally follow the order of the spelling rules as set out in the Spelling Appendix of the National Curriculum and include any words that are specified in the word lists and the non-statutory guidance.

In the second section, 12 half-termly tests are provided, offering two test options per half term: Test A and Test B. These tests offer an equivalent level of challenge and are designed to cover the spelling patterns for that half term's work. The spellings in the half-termly tests are presented in a random order within contextualised sentences. The sentences used are appropriate for the year group in terms of content, grammar and punctuation. The tests are designed to build experience and confidence with this format as well as to test children's spelling knowledge when writing in context.

Each test should take approximately 15 minutes. Guidance is provided for each test, with instructions to read out to the children and a script. The children write the word in the gap in the sentence on their test.

How to use this book

The tests have been written to ensure smooth progression in children's spelling ability within the book and across the rest of the books in series, enabling them to build on their spelling knowledge and show progress.

Marking the tests

The answers are provided in two formats for ease of use: in context and in short form for quick marking.

Recording progress

You can use the pupil-facing record sheets to provide evidence of the areas in which children have performed well and where they need to focus. A spreadsheet is provided in the downloadable version so results can easily be recorded for your classes, and any gaps in understanding can be identified. The spreadsheet can then be used to inform your next teaching and learning steps.

Editable download

All the files are available in Word and PDF format for you to edit if you wish. Go to collins.co.uk/assessment/downloads to find instructions on how to download. The files are password protected and the password clue is included on the website. You will need to use the clue to locate the password in your book.

Year 4/P5 Word lists – Autumn Half Term 1

Word list 1

build
business
calendar
caught
centre
century
certain
circle
complete
breathe

Word list 2

consider
continue
decide
describe
different
difficult
disappear
early
earth
eight

Word list 3

eighth
enough
exercise
experience
experiment
extreme
famous
favourite
February
forward

Year 4/P5 Word lists – Autumn Half Term 1

Word list 4

fruit
grammar
group
guard
guide
heard
heart
height
history
imagine

Word list 5

increase
important
interest
island
knowledge
learn
length
library
material
medicine

© HarperCollins*Publishers* Ltd 2018

Year 4/P5 Word lists – Autumn Half Term 2

Word list 6

mention
minute
natural
naughty
notice
occasion
occasionally
often
opposite
ordinary

Word list 7

particular
peculiar
perhaps
popular
position
possess
possession
possible
potatoes
pressure

Word list 8

probably
promise
purpose
quarter
question
recent
regular
reign
remember
sentence

Year 4/P5 Word lists – Autumn Half Term 2

Word list 9

separate
special
straight
strange
strength
suppose
surprise
therefore
though
although

Word list 10

thought
through
various
weight
woman
women
busy
business
equal
breath

Year 4/P5 Word lists – Spring Half Term 1

Word list 1

disappoint
disagree
disobey
dishonest
disappear
dislike
disbelief
disrespect
distrust
dismount

Word list 2

misbehave
mislead
misspell
mistrust
misheard
misjudge
misfortune
inactive
incorrect
insole

Word list 3

illegal
illegible
immature
immortal
impossible
impatient
imperfect
irregular
irrelevant
irresponsible

Year 4/P5 Word lists – Spring Half Term 1

Word list 4

redo
refresh
return
reappear
redecorate
reapply
repaint
retake
rearrange
replay

Word list 5

subdivide
subheading
submarine
submerge
subway
subtitle
subtotal
superman
superstar
supermarket

Year 4/P5 Word lists – Spring Half Term 2

Word list 6

interact
intercity
international
interrelated
intertwine
antiseptic
antisocial
anticlockwise
autograph
autobiography

Word list 7

measure
treasure
pleasure
enclosure
leisure
creature
furniture
picture
nature
adventure

Word list 8

division
invasion
confusion
decision
collision
television
explosion
vision
revision
mission

Year 4/P5 Word lists – Spring Half Term 2

Word list 9

poison
poisonous
danger
dangerous
mountain
mountainous
fame
famous
vary
various

Word list 10

tremendous
enormous
jealous
delicious
serious
curious
hideous
courteous
obvious
spontaneous

Year 4/P5 Word lists – Summer Half Term 1

Word list 1	Word list 2	Word list 3
humour	invent	express
humorous	invention	expression
glamour	inject	discuss
glamorous	injection	discussion
vigour	act	confess
vigorous	action	confession
courage	hesitate	permit
courageous	hesitation	permission
outrage	complete	admit
outrageous	completion	admission

© HarperCollins*Publishers* Ltd 2018

Year 4/P5 Word lists – Summer Half Term 1

Word list 4

expand
expansion
extend
extension
comprehend
comprehension
attend
attention
intend
intention

Word list 5

music
musician
electric
electrician
magic
magician
politics
politician
mathematic
mathematician

Year 4/P5 Word lists – Summer Half Term 2

Word list 6

scheme
chorus
chemist
echo
character
chef
chalet
machine
brochure
crochet

Word list 7

league
tongue
plague
vague
catalogue
colleague
dialogue
antique
unique
mosque

Word list 8

science
scene
discipline
fascinate
crescent
scissors
descend
muscle
scent
scenery

Year 4/P5 Word lists – Summer Half Term 2

Word list 9

vein
weigh
eight
neighbour
reign
weight
they
obey
prey
grey

Word list 10

accident
accidentally
actual
actually
address
answer
appear
arrive
believe
bicycle

Year 4/P5 Autumn Half Term 1 Test A

Spelling rules and knowledge

- Word list – Years 3 and 4

Guidance for teachers

The test is designed to build experience and confidence with this format, as well as to test children's spelling knowledge.
The test should take approximately 15 minutes.
Children should have a copy of the test and a pencil to use.
Children with specific needs should be given appropriate support.
All children should be encouraged to have a go at spelling each word, using the strategies that they have learnt.
Remind the children to check their answers by asking: *Does it look right? Does it sound right?*
Avoid over-emphasising the spelling of each word as you read it.

> Read each word aloud, saying: *The word is…*
> Next, read the sentence that includes the word.
> Wait for the children to attempt to write the word.
> Re-read the word, saying: *The word is…*

Remind the children to check the word before moving to the next spelling.
At the end of the test, read each sentence again and encourage the children to check back.

Instructions for children

(You may like to read this to the children prior to the test.)

This is a spelling test to check your knowledge of the spelling patterns we have worked on this half term.
You need a pencil.
Please write your name, class and the date at the top of the test.
I will read a word out loud and then say it again in a sentence.
You should write the word in the gap in the sentence on your test.
I will read it again and give you time to check it.
Don't worry if you are not sure about a spelling. Have a go using the strategies we have learnt.
If you make a mistake, cross out the word and try again.

Words tested (20)

circle, difficult, February, imagine, learn, build, continue, enough, guard, important, certain, early, experiment, height, knowledge, calendar, eight, famous, history, library

Year 4/P5 Autumn Half Term 1 Test A

Spelling script

Spelling 1: The word is **circle**.
Stand in a **circle** and hold hands.
The word is **circle**.

Spelling 2: The word is **difficult**.
The spellings became more **difficult** as the children got older.
The word is **difficult**.

Spelling 3: The word is **February**.
In England in **February**, it is likely to be cold.
The word is **February**.

Spelling 4: The word is **imagine**.
Close your eyes and **imagine** you are relaxing on a sandy beach.
The word is **imagine**.

Spelling 5: The word is **learn**.
We have to **learn** our times tables.
The word is **learn**.

Spelling 6: The word is **build**.
We love to **build** sand sculptures.
The word is **build**.

Spelling 7: The word is **continue**.
Please **continue** to read the book in silence.
The word is **continue**.

Spelling 8: The word is **enough**.
When you have eaten **enough** pasta, please clear the table.
The word is **enough**.

Spelling 9: The word is **guard**.
The **guard** dog snarled and bared its teeth.
The word is **guard**.

Spelling 10: The word is **important**.
She carried the **important** message to the office.
The word is **important**.

Spelling 11: The word is **certain**.
I am **certain** that I asked you to brush your hair!
The word is **certain**.

Spelling 12: The word is **early**.
We like to be **early** for the bus.
The word is **early**.

Spelling 13: The word is **experiment**.
The scientist's **experiment** went drastically wrong.
The word is **experiment**.

Spelling 14: The word is **height**.
The **height** of the tower made me feel giddy.
The word is **height**.

Spelling 15: The word is **knowledge**.
His **knowledge** of international football players was extraordinary.
The word is **knowledge**.

Spelling 16: The word is **calendar**.
Please add the girls' birthdays to the **calendar**.
The word is **calendar**.

Spelling 17: The word is **eight**.
Spiders usually have **eight** legs.
The word is **eight**.

Spelling 18: The word is **famous**.
The world-**famous** opera singer bowed to the applause.
The word is **famous**.

Spelling 19: The word is **history**.
We can learn about our local **history** by looking at the local buildings.
The word is **history**.

Spelling 20: The word is **library**.
We visit the **library** to borrow interesting books.
The word is **library**.

Well done! Now I will read the sentences again so you can check your spelling.

| Name | Class | Date |

Year 4/P5 Autumn Half Term 1 Test A

1. Stand in a _____ and hold hands.

2. The spellings became more _____ as the children got older.

3. In England in _____, it is likely to be cold.

4. Close your eyes and _____ you are relaxing on a sandy beach.

5. We have to _____ our times tables.

6. We love to _____ sand sculptures.

7. Please _____ to read the book in silence.

8. When you have eaten _____ pasta, please clear the table.

9. The _____ dog snarled and bared its teeth.

10. She carried the _____ message to the office.

11. I am _____ that I asked you to brush your hair!

12. We like to be _____ for the bus.

13. The scientist's _____ went drastically wrong.

14. The _____ of the tower made me feel giddy.

15. His _____ of international football players was extraordinary.

16. Please add the girls' birthdays to the _____.

17. Spiders usually have _____ legs.

18. The world-_____ opera singer bowed to the applause.

19. We can learn about our local _____ by looking at the local buildings.

20. We visit the _____ to borrow interesting books.

Total _____ / 20

Year 4/P5 Autumn Half Term 1 Test B

Spelling rules and knowledge

- Word list – Years 3 and 4

Guidance for teachers

The test is designed to build experience and confidence with this format, as well as to test children's spelling knowledge.
The test should take approximately 15 minutes.
Children should have a copy of the test and a pencil to use.
Children with specific needs should be given appropriate support.
All children should be encouraged to have a go at spelling each word, using the strategies that they have learnt.
Remind the children to check their answers by asking: *Does it look right? Does it sound right?*
Avoid over-emphasising the spelling of each word as you read it.

> Read each word aloud, saying: *The word is…*
> Next, read the sentence that includes the word.
> Wait for the children to attempt to write the word.
> Re-read the word, saying: *The word is…*

Remind the children to check the word before moving to the next spelling.
At the end of the test, read each sentence again and encourage the children to check back.

Instructions for children

(You may like to read this to the children prior to the test.)

This is a spelling test to check your knowledge of the spelling patterns we have worked on this half term.
You need a pencil.
Please write your name, class and the date at the top of the test.
I will read a word out loud and then say it again in a sentence.
You should write the word in the gap in the sentence on your test.
I will read it again and give you time to check it.
Don't worry if you are not sure about a spelling. Have a go using the strategies we have learnt.
If you make a mistake, cross out the word and try again.

Words tested (20)

century, earth, exercise, fruit, island, breathe, disappear, favourite, heart, material, business, decide, experience, guide, interest, centre, consider, extreme, group, increase

Year 4/P5 Autumn Half Term 1 Test B

Spelling script

Spelling 1: The word is **century**.
How many years are there in a **century**?
The word is **century**.

Spelling 2: The word is **earth**.
The **earth** spins on its own axis every day.
The word is **earth**.

Spelling 3: The word is **exercise**.
We **exercise** to keep our hearts strong and healthy.
The word is **exercise**.

Spelling 4: The word is **fruit**.
Pineapple is a delicious yellow **fruit**.
The word is **fruit**.

Spelling 5: The word is **island**.
The pirates landed on Treasure **Island**.
The word is **island**.

Spelling 6: The word is **breathe**.
We **breathe** air into our lungs.
The word is **breathe**.

Spelling 7: The word is **disappear**.
Please don't **disappear** when I need you!
The word is **disappear**.

Spelling 8: The word is **favourite**.
Cola is my **favourite** fizzy drink.
The word is **favourite**.

Spelling 9: The word is **heart**.
How many times does your **heart** beat each minute?
The word is **heart**.

Spelling 10: The word is **material**.
We had to sort each different **material** in science.
The word is **material**.

Spelling 11: The word is **business**.
He told us to mind our own **business**!
The word is **business**.

Spelling 12: The word is **decide**.
I can't **decide** between cake and ice cream.
The word is **decide**.

Spelling 13: The word is **experience**.
Riding the zip-wire was a thrilling **experience**.
The word is **experience**.

Spelling 14: The word is **guide**.
The **guide** led us around the ruined temple.
The word is **guide**.

Spelling 15: The word is **interest**.
The boy's **interest** in birdwatching was obvious.
The word is **interest**.

Spelling 16: The word is **centre**.
Stand in the **centre** of the circle and spin three times.
The word is **centre**.

Spelling 17: The word is **consider**.
Please **consider** what you would like to do when you grow up.
The word is **consider**.

Spelling 18: The word is **extreme**.
The **extreme** conditions meant we couldn't climb the mountain.
The word is **extreme**.

Spelling 19: The word is **group**.
The **group** of monkeys raced after the bananas.
The word is **group**.

Spelling 20: The word is **increase**.
I would love my pocket money to **increase**!
The word is **increase**.

Well done! Now I will read the sentences again so you can check your spelling.

| Name | Class | Date |

Year 4/P5 Autumn Half Term 1 Test B

1. How many years are there in a _____?

2. The _____ spins on its own axis every day.

3. We _____ to keep our hearts strong and healthy.

4. Pineapple is a delicious yellow _____.

5. The pirates landed on Treasure _____.

6. We _____ air into our lungs.

7. Please don't _____ when I need you!

8. Cola is my _____ fizzy drink.

9. How many times does your _____ beat each minute?

10. We had to sort each different _____ in science.

11. He told us to mind our own _____!

12. I can't _____ between cake and ice cream.

13. Riding the zip-wire was a thrilling _____.

14. The _____ led us around the ruined temple.

15. The boy's _____ in birdwatching was obvious.

16. Stand in the _____ of the circle and spin three times.

17. Please _____ what you would like to do when you grow up.

18. The _____ conditions meant we couldn't climb the mountain.

19. The _____ of monkeys raced after the bananas.

20. I would love my pocket money to _____!

Total _____ / 20

Year 4/P5 Autumn Half Term 2 Test A

Spelling rules and knowledge

- Word list – Years 3 and 4

Guidance for teachers

The test is designed to build experience and confidence with this format, as well as to test children's spelling knowledge.
The test should take approximately 15 minutes.
Children should have a copy of the test and a pencil to use.
Children with specific needs should be given appropriate support.
All children should be encouraged to have a go at spelling each word, using the strategies that they have learnt.
Remind the children to check their answers by asking: *Does it look right? Does it sound right?*
Avoid over-emphasising the spelling of each word as you read it.

> Read each word aloud, saying: *The word is…*
> Next, read the sentence that includes the word.
> Wait for the children to attempt to write the word.
> Re-read the word, saying: *The word is…*

Remind the children to check the word before moving to the next spelling.
At the end of the test, read each sentence again and encourage the children to check back.

Instructions for children

(You may like to read this to the children prior to the test.)

This is a spelling test to check your knowledge of the spelling patterns we have worked on this half term.
You need a pencil.
Please write your name, class and the date at the top of the test.
I will read a word out loud and then say it again in a sentence.
You should write the word in the gap in the sentence on your test.
I will read it again and give you time to check it.
Don't worry if you are not sure about a spelling. Have a go using the strategies we have learnt.
If you make a mistake, cross out the word and try again.

Words tested (20)

ordinary, perhaps, remember, although, busy, naughty, peculiar, quarter, separate, thought, occasion, position, regular, strange, women, minute, popular, purpose, suppose, breath

Year 4/P5 Autumn Half Term 2 Test A

Spelling script

Spelling 1: The word is **ordinary**.
Today was no **ordinary** day!
The word is **ordinary**.

Spelling 2: The word is **perhaps**.
Perhaps you would like to see a film tonight?
The word is **perhaps**.

Spelling 3: The word is **remember**.
Can you **remember** learning to write your name?
The word is **remember**.

Spelling 4: The word is **although**.
Although he was tired, he managed to stay awake for the party.
The word is **although**.

Spelling 5: The word is **busy**.
Let's make ourselves **busy** so we don't feel bored.
The word is **busy**.

Spelling 6: The word is **naughty**.
The **naughty** monkey loved to play tricks.
The word is **naughty**.

Spelling 7: The word is **peculiar**.
Spinning around can give you a **peculiar** sensation.
The word is **peculiar**.

Spelling 8: The word is **quarter**.
Some children start school at **quarter** to nine.
The word is **quarter**.

Spelling 9: The word is **separate**.
Can you **separate** the egg yolk from the white?
The word is **separate**.

Spelling 10: The word is **thought**.
He **thought** really hard before choosing his gift.
The word is **thought**.

Spelling 11: The word is **occasion**.
The wedding was a joyful **occasion**.
The word is **occasion**.

Spelling 12: The word is **position**.
Which **position** would you like to play in today?
The word is **position**.

Spelling 13: The word is regular.
I always order a regular sized drink.
The word is regular.

Spelling 14: The word is strange.
The strange smell wafted through the room.
The word is strange.

Spelling 15: The word is women.
Some women drove army vehicles during the Second World War.
The word is women.

Spelling 16: The word is minute.
In a minute, we will be able to go out to play.
The word is minute.

Spelling 17: The word is popular.
Rabbits are popular pets for children.
The word is popular.

Spelling 18: The word is purpose.
He forgot his PE bag on purpose.
The word is purpose.

Spelling 19: The word is suppose.
I suppose you would like to share my sweets?
The word is suppose.

Spelling 20: The word is breath.
She took a deep breath before diving in.
The word is breath.

Well done! Now I will read the sentences again so you can check your spelling.

| Name | Class | Date |

Year 4/P5 Autumn Half Term 2 Test A

1. Today was no _____ day!

2. _____ you would like to see a film tonight?

3. Can you _____ learning to write your name?

4. _____ he was tired, he managed to stay awake for the party.

5. Let's make ourselves _____ so we don't feel bored.

6. The _____ monkey loved to play tricks.

7. Spinning around can give you a _____ sensation.

8. Some children start school at _____ to nine.

9. Can you _____ the egg yolk from the white?

10. He _____ really hard before choosing his gift.

11. The wedding was a joyful _____.

12. Which _____ would you like to play in today?

13. I always order a _____ sized drink.

14. The _____ smell wafted through the room.

15. Some _____ drove army vehicles during the Second World War.

16. In a _____, we will be able to go out to play.

17. Rabbits are _____ pets for children.

18. He forgot his PE bag on _____.

19. I _____ you would like to share my sweets?

20. She took a deep _____ before diving in.

Total _____ / 20

Year 4/P5 Autumn Half Term 2 Test B

Spelling rules and knowledge

- Word list – Years 3 and 4

Guidance for teachers

The test is designed to build experience and confidence with this format, as well as to test children's spelling knowledge.
The test should take approximately 15 minutes.
Children should have a copy of the test and a pencil to use.
Children with specific needs should be given appropriate support.
All children should be encouraged to have a go at spelling each word, using the strategies that they have learnt.
Remind the children to check their answers by asking: *Does it look right? Does it sound right?*
Avoid over-emphasising the spelling of each word as you read it.

> Read each word aloud, saying: *The word is…*
> Next, read the sentence that includes the word.
> Wait for the children to attempt to write the word.
> Re-read the word, saying: *The word is…*

Remind the children to check the word before moving to the next spelling.
At the end of the test, read each sentence again and encourage the children to check back.

Instructions for children

(You may like to read this to the children prior to the test.)

This is a spelling test to check your knowledge of the spelling patterns we have worked on this half term.
You need a pencil.
Please write your name, class and the date at the top of the test.
I will read a word out loud and then say it again in a sentence.
You should write the word in the gap in the sentence on your test.
I will read it again and give you time to check it.
Don't worry if you are not sure about a spelling. Have a go using the strategies we have learnt.
If you make a mistake, cross out the word and try again.

Words tested (20)

natural, potatoes, probably, special, through, opposite, possible, question, surprise, equal, notice, possess, recent, though, woman, mention, particular, promise, straight, various

Year 4/P5 Autumn Half Term 2 Test B

Spelling script

Spelling 1: The word is **natural**.
She was a **natural** swimmer.
The word is **natural**.

Spelling 2: The word is **potatoes**.
We mash **potatoes** with butter and cream.
The word is **potatoes**.

Spelling 3: The word is **probably**.
She will **probably** arrive early.
The word is **probably**.

Spelling 4: The word is **special**.
He liked to drink his tea from a **special** cup.
The word is **special**.

Spelling 5: The word is **through**.
They wriggled **through** the gap in the fence and into the woods.
The word is **through**.

Spelling 6: The word is **opposite**.
What is the **opposite** of hot?
The word is **opposite**.

Spelling 7: The word is **possible**.
Would it be **possible** for my child to stand in front of you?
The word is **possible**.

Spelling 8: The word is **question**.
I am sure you can answer this **question**.
The word is **question**.

Spelling 9: The word is **surprise**.
The beautiful flowers were a lovely **surprise** for Mum.
The word is **surprise**.

Spelling 10: The word is **equal**.
We shared the sweets into two **equal** piles.
The word is **equal**.

Spelling 11: The word is **notice**.
The police officer didn't **notice** the car as it jumped the red light.
The word is **notice**.

Spelling 12: The word is **possess**.
We don't **possess** enough information to decide who should win.
The word is **possess**.

Spelling 13: The word is **recent**.
The most **recent** addition to their collection of pets was a baby hamster.
The word is **recent**.

Spelling 14: The word is **though**.
Even **though** the water was chilly, we dived in.
The word is **though**.

Spelling 15: The word is **woman**.
The super-fit elderly **woman** cycled up the hill and overtook the young cyclist.
The word is **woman**.

Spelling 16: The word is **mention**.
Please don't **mention** the spot on my nose!
The word is **mention**.

Spelling 17: The word is **particular**.
She was **particular** about what she would eat.
The word is **particular**.

Spelling 18: The word is **promise**.
I said I would never break a **promise**.
The word is **promise**.

Spelling 19: The word is **straight**.
Roman roads were usually long and **straight**.
The word is **straight**.

Spelling 20: The word is **various**.
The plants were grown in pots of **various** sizes.
The word is **various**.

Well done! Now I will read the sentences again so you can check your spelling.

| Name | Class | Date |

Year 4/P5 Autumn Half Term 2 Test B

1. She was a _____ swimmer.

2. We mash _____ with butter and cream.

3. She will _____ arrive early.

4. He liked to drink his tea from a _____ cup.

5. They wriggled _____ the gap in the fence and into the woods.

6. What is the _____ of hot?

7. Would it be _____ for my child to stand in front of you?

8. I am sure you can answer this _____.

9. The beautiful flowers were a lovely _____ for Mum.

10. We shared the sweets into two _____ piles.

11. The police officer didn't _____ the car as it jumped the red light.

12. We don't _____ enough information to decide who should win.

13. The most _____ addition to their collection of pets was a baby hamster.

14. Even _____ the water was chilly, we dived in.

15. The super-fit elderly _____ cycled up the hill and overtook the young cyclist.

16. Please don't _____ the spot on my nose!

17. She was _____ about what she would eat.

18. I said I would never break a _____.

19. Roman roads were usually long and _____.

20. The plants were grown in pots of _____ sizes.

Total _____ / 20

Year 4/P5 Spring Half Term 1 Test A

Spelling rules and knowledge

- Prefixes (**dis-**, **mis-**, **in-**, **im-**, **il-**, **ir-**, **re-**, **sub-**, **inter-**, **super-**)

Guidance for teachers

The test is designed to build experience and confidence with this format, as well as to test children's spelling knowledge.
The test should take approximately 15 minutes.
Children should have a copy of the test and a pencil to use.
Children with specific needs should be given appropriate support.
All children should be encouraged to have a go at spelling each word, using the strategies that they have learnt.
Remind the children to check their answers by asking: *Does it look right? Does it sound right?*
Avoid over-emphasising the spelling of each word as you read it.

> Read each word aloud, saying: *The word is…*
> Next, read the sentence that includes the word.
> Wait for the children to attempt to write the word.
> Re-read the word, saying: *The word is…*

Remind the children to check the word before moving to the next spelling.
At the end of the test, read each sentence again and encourage the children to check back.

Instructions for children

(You may like to read this to the children prior to the test.)

This is a spelling test to check your knowledge of the spelling patterns we have worked on this half term.
You need a pencil.
Please write your name, class and the date at the top of the test.
I will read a word out loud and then say it again in a sentence.
You should write the word in the gap in the sentence on your test.
I will read it again and give you time to check it.
Don't worry if you are not sure about a spelling. Have a go using the strategies we have learnt.
If you make a mistake, cross out the word and try again.

Words tested (20)

disappoint, misheard, impatient, refresh, supermarket, disobey, misbehave, illegal, return, submarine, disappear, misjudge, immature, reapply, submerge, distrust, incorrect, irrelevant, repaint, subdivide

Year 4/P5 Spring Half Term 1 Test A

Spelling script

Spelling 1: The word is **disappoint**.
We tried not to **disappoint** our teacher!
The word is **disappoint**.

Spelling 2: The word is **misheard**.
The old man was slightly deaf so he **misheard** the children.
The word is **misheard**.

Spelling 3: The word is **impatient**.
The coach became **impatient** as he waited for his players to change.
The word is **impatient**.

Spelling 4: The word is **refresh**.
You need to **refresh** the browser to make the search engine work.
The word is **refresh**.

Spelling 5: The word is **supermarket**.
We hate shopping in the **supermarket**.
The word is **supermarket**.

Spelling 6: The word is **disobey**.
The prisoner didn't dare to **disobey** the guard.
The word is **disobey**.

Spelling 7: The word is **misbehave**.
The children tried not to **misbehave** in class.
The word is **misbehave**.

Spelling 8: The word is **illegal**.
It is **illegal** to ride a bicycle on a motorway.
The word is **illegal**.

Spelling 9: The word is **return**.
I need to **return** the faulty television to the shop.
The word is **return**.

Spelling 10: The word is **submarine**.
Life on a **submarine** is very cramped!
The word is **submarine**.

Spelling 11: The word is **disappear**.
He loved to **disappear** just before bedtime!
The word is **disappear**.

Spelling 12: The word is **misjudge**.
Don't **misjudge** a book before reading it.
The word is **misjudge**.

Spelling 13: The word is **immature**.
The little boy seemed **immature** to his older brother.
The word is **immature**.

Spelling 14: The word is **reapply**.
We must **reapply** the paint where it has peeled.
The word is **reapply**.

Spelling 15: The word is **submerge**.
We tried to **submerge** an inflated rubber ring.
The word is **submerge**.

Spelling 16: The word is **distrust**.
The shopkeeper's **distrust** was obvious when he saw the children enter the shop.
The word is **distrust**.

Spelling 17: The word is **incorrect**.
The teacher smiled even though the child's answer was **incorrect**.
The word is **incorrect**.

Spelling 18: The word is **irrelevant**.
Who won the match was **irrelevant** to the proud coach.
The word is **irrelevant**.

Spelling 19: The word is **repaint**.
The girl was desperate to **repaint** her bedroom.
The word is **repaint**.

Spelling 20: The word is **subdivide**.
Fold the paper in half, then **subdivide** it again.
The word is **subdivide**.

Well done! Now I will read the sentences again so you can check your spelling.

| Name | Class | Date |

Year 4/P5 Spring Half Term 1 Test A

1. We tried not to _____ our teacher!

2. The old man was slightly deaf so he _____ the children.

3. The coach became _____ as he waited for his players to change.

4. You need to _____ the browser to make the search engine work.

5. We hate shopping in the _____.

6. The prisoner didn't dare to _____ the guard.

7. The children tried not to _____ in class.

8. It is _____ to ride a bicycle on a motorway.

9. I need to _____ the faulty television to the shop.

10. Life on a _____ is very cramped!

11. He loved to _____ just before bedtime!

12. Don't _____ a book before reading it.

13. The little boy seemed _____ to his older brother.

14. We must _____ the paint where it has peeled.

15. We tried to _____ an inflated rubber ring.

16. The shopkeeper's _____ was obvious when he saw the children enter the shop.

17. The teacher smiled even though the child's answer was _____.

18. Who won the match was _____ to the proud coach.

19. The girl was desperate to _____ her bedroom.

20. Fold the paper in half, then _____ it again.

Total _____ **/ 20**

Year 4/P5 Spring Half Term 1 Test B

Spelling rules and knowledge

- Prefixes (**dis-**, **mis-**, **in-**, **im-**, **il-**, **ir-**, **re-**, **sub-**, **inter-**, **super-**)

Guidance for teachers

The test is designed to build experience and confidence with this format, as well as to test children's spelling knowledge.
The test should take approximately 15 minutes.
Children should have a copy of the test and a pencil to use.
Children with specific needs should be given appropriate support.
All children should be encouraged to have a go at spelling each word, using the strategies that they have learnt.
Remind the children to check their answers by asking: *Does it look right? Does it sound right?*
Avoid over-emphasising the spelling of each word as you read it.

>Read each word aloud, saying: *The word is…*
>Next, read the sentence that includes the word.
>Wait for the children to attempt to write the word.
>Re-read the word, saying: *The word is…*

Remind the children to check the word before moving to the next spelling.
At the end of the test, read each sentence again and encourage the children to check back.

Instructions for children

(You may like to read this to the children prior to the test.)

This is a spelling test to check your knowledge of the spelling patterns we have worked on this half term.
You need a pencil.
Please write your name, class and the date at the top of the test.
I will read a word out loud and then say it again in a sentence.
You should write the word in the gap in the sentence on your test.
I will read it again and give you time to check it.
Don't worry if you are not sure about a spelling. Have a go using the strategies we have learnt.
If you make a mistake, cross out the word and try again.

Words tested (20)

disagree, mislead, imperfect, replay, subtotal, dislike, inactive, impossible, rearrange, superstar, dishonest, misspell, illegible, retake, subtitle, dismount, misfortune, irresponsible, redecorate, subway

Year 4/P5 Spring Half Term 1 Test B

Spelling script

Spelling 1: The word is **disagree**.
Would anyone like to **disagree** with the argument?
The word is **disagree**.

Spelling 2: The word is **mislead**.
News reports can **mislead** you.
The word is **mislead**.

Spelling 3: The word is **imperfect**.
The china cup was **imperfect** and had to be returned to the shop.
The word is **imperfect**.

Spelling 4: The word is **replay**.
Can you **replay** the video and watch it again?
The word is **replay**.

Spelling 5: The word is **subtotal**.
The **subtotal** on the bill was £35.00.
The word is **subtotal**.

Spelling 6: The word is **dislike**.
Many children **dislike** aubergines.
The word is **dislike**.

Spelling 7: The word is **inactive**.
Research proves that it is unhealthy to be **inactive** for too long each day.
The word is **inactive**.

Spelling 8: The word is **impossible**.
It was **impossible** to stop the snowman from melting.
The word is **impossible**.

Spelling 9: The word is **rearrange**.
Why don't you **rearrange** your bedroom?
The word is **rearrange**.

Spelling 10: The word is **superstar**.
Every talent show has a **superstar**.
The word is **superstar**.

Spelling 11: The word is **dishonest**.
No-one trusted the **dishonest** cyclist.
The word is **dishonest**.

Spelling 12: The word is **misspell**.
It is easy to **misspell** words with prefixes!
The word is **misspell**.

Spelling 13: The word is **illegible**.
The old man's hand shook so his handwriting was **illegible**.
The word is **illegible**.

Spelling 14: The word is **retake**.
She had to **retake** the selfie.
The word is **retake**.

Spelling 15: The word is **subtitle**.
In a book, a **subtitle** can give the reader more information about the content.
The word is **subtitle**.

Spelling 16: The word is **dismount**.
The rider struggled to **dismount** from her horse.
The word is **dismount**.

Spelling 17: The word is **misfortune**.
They had the **misfortune** to lose their tortoise.
The word is **misfortune**.

Spelling 18: The word is **irresponsible**.
The **irresponsible** boy forgot his homework.
The word is **irresponsible**.

Spelling 19: The word is **redecorate**.
We can **redecorate** in any colour we want!
The word is **redecorate**.

Spelling 20: The word is **subway**.
We use the **subway** to reach the other side of the busy road safely.
The word is **subway**.

Well done! Now I will read the sentences again so you can check your spelling.

| Name | Class | Date |

Year 4/P5 Spring Half Term 1 Test B

1. Would anyone like to _____ with the argument?

2. News reports can _____ you.

3. The china cup was _____ and had to be returned to the shop.

4. Can you _____ the video and watch it again?

5. The _____ on the bill was £35.00.

6. Many children _____ aubergines.

7. Research proves that it is unhealthy to be _____ for too long each day.

8. It was _____ to stop the snowman from melting.

9. Why don't you _____ your bedroom?

10. Every talent show has a _____.

11. No-one trusted the _____ cyclist.

12. It is easy to _____ words with prefixes!

13. The old man's hand shook so his handwriting was _____.

14. She had to _____ the selfie.

15. In a book, a _____ can give the reader more information about the content.

16. The rider struggled to _____ from her horse.

17. They had the _____ to lose their tortoise.

18. The _____ boy forgot his homework.

19. We can _____ in any colour we want!

20. We use the _____ to reach the other side of the busy road safely.

Total _____ / 20

Year 4/P5 Spring Half Term 2 Test A

Spelling rules and knowledge

- Prefixes (**anti-**, **auto-**)
- The sound made by **-sure** at the end of a word
- The sound made by **-sion** at the end of a word
- The suffix **-ous**

Guidance for teachers

The test is designed to build experience and confidence with this format, as well as to test children's spelling knowledge.
The test should take approximately 15 minutes.
Children should have a copy of the test and a pencil to use.
Children with specific needs should be given appropriate support.
All children should be encouraged to have a go at spelling each word, using the strategies that they have learnt.
Remind the children to check their answers by asking: *Does it look right? Does it sound right?*
Avoid over-emphasising the spelling of each word as you read it.

> Read each word aloud, saying: *The word is…*
> Next, read the sentence that includes the word.
> Wait for the children to attempt to write the word.
> Re-read the word, saying: *The word is…*

Remind the children to check the word before moving to the next spelling.
At the end of the test, read each sentence again and encourage the children to check back.

Instructions for children

(You may like to read this to the children prior to the test.)

This is a spelling test to check your knowledge of the spelling patterns we have worked on this half term.
You need a pencil.
Please write your name, class and the date at the top of the test.
I will read a word out loud and then say it again in a sentence.
You should write the word in the gap in the sentence on your test.
I will read it again and give you time to check it.
Don't worry if you are not sure about a spelling. Have a go using the strategies we have learnt.
If you make a mistake, cross out the word and try again.

Words tested (20)

anticlockwise, nature, vision, dangerous, jealous, intercity, measure, decision, poisonous, enormous, autobiography, creature, television, spontaneous, tremendous, international, treasure, revision, courteous, hideous

© HarperCollins*Publishers* Ltd 2018

Year 4/P5 Spring Half Term 2 Test A

Spelling script

Spelling 1: The word is **anticlockwise**.
The magical clock's hands moved in an **anticlockwise** direction.
The word is **anticlockwise**.

Spelling 2: The word is **nature**.
The children loved to explore the **nature** around them.
The word is **nature**.

Spelling 3: The word is **vision**.
Aeroplane pilots need perfect **vision**.
The word is **vision**.

Spelling 4: The word is **dangerous**.
The busy road was known for being **dangerous**.
The word is **dangerous**.

Spelling 5: The word is **jealous**.
She was **jealous** of her friend's pierced ears.
The word is **jealous**.

Spelling 6: The word is **intercity**.
We took the **intercity** train to Glasgow.
The word is **intercity**.

Spelling 7: The word is **measure**.
Please **measure** the hall with a metre stick.
The word is **measure**.

Spelling 8: The word is **decision**.
The teacher's **decision** was final.
The word is **decision**.

Spelling 9: The word is **poisonous**.
The **poisonous** viper had beautiful markings.
The word is **poisonous**.

Spelling 10: The word is **enormous**.
The **enormous** garden gnome toppled into the pond with a splash.
The word is **enormous**.

Spelling 11: The word is **autobiography**.
Sports people often write their **autobiography**.
The word is **autobiography**.

Spelling 12: The word is **creature**.
The glimmering scaly **creature** emerged from beneath the waves.
The word is **creature**.

Spelling 13: The word is **television**.
I would love a **television** in my bedroom!
The word is **television**.

Spelling 14: The word is **spontaneous**.
Jumping into the freezing river was a **spontaneous** action.
The word is **spontaneous**.

Spelling 15: The word is **tremendous**.
The children gave a **tremendous** cheer as their head teacher finished the race.
The word is **tremendous**.

Spelling 16: The word is **international**.
The **international** airport was always busy.
The word is **international**.

Spelling 17: The word is **treasure**.
I dream of finding **treasure** on a faraway island.
The word is **treasure**.

Spelling 18: The word is **revision**.
The girls had to do **revision** at the weekend.
The word is **revision**.

Spelling 19: The word is **courteous**.
The **courteous** boy held the door open for us.
The word is **courteous**.

Spelling 20: The word is **hideous**.
The **hideous** weather stopped us from going camping at half term.
The word is **hideous**.

Well done! Now I will read the sentences again so you can check your spelling.

| Name | Class | Date |

Year 4/P5 Spring Half Term 2 Test A

1. The magical clock's hands moved in an _____ direction.

2. The children loved to explore the _____ around them.

3. Aeroplane pilots need perfect _____.

4. The busy road was known for being _____.

5. She was _____ of her friend's pierced ears.

6. We took the _____ train to Glasgow.

7. Please _____ the hall with a metre stick.

8. The teacher's _____ was final.

9. The _____ viper had beautiful markings.

10. The _____ garden gnome toppled into the pond with a splash.

11. Sports people often write their _____.

12. The glimmering scaly _____ emerged from beneath the waves.

13. I would love a _____ in my bedroom!

14. Jumping into the freezing river was a _____ action.

15. The children gave a _____ cheer as their head teacher finished the race.

16. The _____ airport was always busy.

17. I dream of finding _____ on a faraway island.

18. The girls had to do _____ at the weekend.

19. The _____ boy held the door open for us.

20. The _____ weather stopped us from going camping at half term.

Total _____ / 20

Year 4/P5 Spring Half Term 2 Test B

Spelling rules and knowledge

- Prefixes (**anti-**, **auto-**)
- The sound made by **-sure** at the end of a word
- The sound made by **-sion** at the end of a word
- The suffix **-ous**

Guidance for teachers

The test is designed to build experience and confidence with this format, as well as to test children's spelling knowledge.
The test should take approximately 15 minutes.
Children should have a copy of the test and a pencil to use.
Children with specific needs should be given appropriate support.
All children should be encouraged to have a go at spelling each word, using the strategies that they have learnt.
Remind the children to check their answers by asking: *Does it look right? Does it sound right?*
Avoid over-emphasising the spelling of each word as you read it.

> Read each word aloud, saying: *The word is…*
> Next, read the sentence that includes the word.
> Wait for the children to attempt to write the word.
> Re-read the word, saying: *The word is…*

Remind the children to check the word before moving to the next spelling.
At the end of the test, read each sentence again and encourage the children to check back.

Instructions for children

(You may like to read this to the children prior to the test.)

This is a spelling test to check your knowledge of the spelling patterns we have worked on this half term.
You need a pencil.
Please write your name, class and the date at the top of the test.
I will read a word out loud and then say it again in a sentence.
You should write the word in the gap in the sentence on your test.
I will read it again and give you time to check it.
Don't worry if you are not sure about a spelling. Have a go using the strategies we have learnt.
If you make a mistake, cross out the word and try again.

Words tested (20)

antiseptic, pleasure, collision, mountainous, obvious, autograph, picture, explosion, famous, delicious, intertwine, furniture, confusion, cautious, serious, antisocial, leisure, division, curious, various

© HarperCollins*Publishers* Ltd 2018

Year 4/P5 Spring Half Term 2 Test B

Spelling script

Spelling 1: The word is **antiseptic**.
Mum used **antiseptic** on my grazed knee.
The word is **antiseptic**.

Spelling 2: The word is **pleasure**.
It was a **pleasure** to see my cousins.
The word is **pleasure**.

Spelling 3: The word is **collision**.
The **collision** left the driver shaken.
The word is **collision**.

Spelling 4: The word is **mountainous**.
Wales is a **mountainous** country.
The word is **mountainous**.

Spelling 5: The word is **obvious**.
The solution to the problem was **obvious**.
The word is **obvious**.

Spelling 6: The word is **autograph**.
I asked the pop star for her **autograph**.
The word is **autograph**.

Spelling 7: The word is **picture**.
He took a **picture** with his mobile phone.
The word is **picture**.

Spelling 8: The word is **explosion**.
Shortly after the **explosion**, the fire engine arrived.
The word is **explosion**.

Spelling 9: The word is **famous**.
We want to see the **famous** singer.
The word is **famous**.

Spelling 10: The word is **delicious**.
The chocolate cake was absolutely **delicious**.
The word is **delicious**.

Spelling 11: The word is **intertwine**.
Can you **intertwine** your fingers?
The word is **intertwine**.

Spelling 12: The word is **furniture**.
We moved the **furniture** to look for the gerbil.
The word is **furniture**.

Spelling 13: The word is **confusion**.
She caused **confusion** by arriving a day early for the meeting.
The word is **confusion**.

Spelling 14: The word is **cautious**.
We were **cautious** when we held the tarantula.
The word is **cautious**.

Spelling 15: The word is **serious**.
The **serious** gentleman's face broke into a smile.
The word is **serious**.

Spelling 16: The word is **antisocial**.
He felt **antisocial** so he didn't go to the party.
The word is **antisocial**.

Spelling 17: The word is **leisure**.
We can do trampolining at the **leisure** centre.
The word is **leisure**.

Spelling 18: The word is **division**.
Division problems can be trickier than multiplication problems.
The word is **division**.

Spelling 19: The word is **curious**.
The **curious** cat peered at its reflection in the pond.
The word is **curious**.

Spelling 20: The word is **various**.
We tried **various** methods to solve the problem.
The word is **various**.

Well done! Now I will read the sentences again so you can check your spelling.

| Name | Class | Date |

Year 4/P5 Spring Half Term 2 Test B

1. Mum used _____ on my grazed knee.

2. It was a _____ to see my cousins.

3. The _____ left the driver shaken.

4. Wales is a _____ country.

5. The solution to the problem was _____.

6. I asked the pop star for her _____.

7. He took a _____ with his mobile phone.

8. Shortly after the _____, the fire engine arrived.

9. We want to see the _____ singer.

10. The chocolate cake was absolutely _____.

11. Can you _____ your fingers?

12. We moved the _____ to look for the gerbil.

13. She caused _____ by arriving a day early for the meeting.

14. We were _____ when we held the tarantula.

15. The _____ gentleman's face broke into a smile.

16. He felt _____ so he didn't go to the party.

17. We can do trampolining at the _____ centre.

18. _____ problems can be trickier than multiplication problems.

19. The _____ cat peered at its reflection in the pond.

20. We tried _____ methods to solve the problem.

Total _____ / 20

Year 4/P5 Summer Half Term 1 Test A

Spelling rules and knowledge

- The suffix **-ous**
- Endings spelt **-tion**, **-tian**, **-sion**, **-cian**, **-ssion**

Guidance for teachers

The test is designed to build experience and confidence with this format, as well as to test children's spelling knowledge.
The test should take approximately 15 minutes.
Children should have a copy of the test and a pencil to use.
Children with specific needs should be given appropriate support.
All children should be encouraged to have a go at spelling each word, using the strategies that they have learnt.
Remind the children to check their answers by asking: *Does it look right? Does it sound right?*
Avoid over-emphasising the spelling of each word as you read it.

> Read each word aloud, saying: *The word is…*
> Next, read the sentence that includes the word.
> Wait for the children to attempt to write the word.
> Re-read the word, saying: *The word is…*

Remind the children to check the word before moving to the next spelling.
At the end of the test, read each sentence again and encourage the children to check back.

Instructions for children

(You may like to read this to the children prior to the test.)

This is a spelling test to check your knowledge of the spelling patterns we have worked on this half term.
You need a pencil.
Please write your name, class and the date at the top of the test.
I will read a word out loud and then say it again in a sentence.
You should write the word in the gap in the sentence on your test.
I will read it again and give you time to check it.
Don't worry if you are not sure about a spelling. Have a go using the strategies we have learnt.
If you make a mistake, cross out the word and try again.

Words tested (20)

courageous, action, admission, comprehension, magician, glamorous, invention, discussion, extension, musician, humorous, exception, confession, intention, beautician, operation, situation, decision, illusion, optician

Year 4/P5 Summer Half Term 1 Test A

Spelling script

Spelling 1: The word is **courageous**.
The **courageous** dog swam to the sinking boat.
The word is **courageous**.

Spelling 2: The word is **action**.
The dance **action** was hard to copy.
The word is **action**.

Spelling 3: The word is **admission**.
Admission to the museum took ages.
The word is **admission**.

Spelling 4: The word is **comprehension**.
At school we do reading **comprehension** tests.
The word is **comprehension**.

Spelling 5: The word is **magician**.
The **magician** waved his wand and disappeared.
The word is **magician**.

Spelling 6: The word is **glamorous**.
The **glamorous** model strutted down the catwalk.
The word is **glamorous**.

Spelling 7: The word is **invention**.
Hybrid cars are a modern **invention**.
The word is **invention**.

Spelling 8: The word is **discussion**.
The **discussion** failed because everyone spoke at once.
The word is **discussion**.

Spelling 9: The word is **extension**.
The **extension** lead was stretched as Dad tried to reach the fence with his drill.
The word is **extension**.

Spelling 10: The word is **musician**.
The **musician** set up his guitar and amp.
The word is **musician**.

Spelling 11: The word is **humorous**.
The most **humorous** moment of the walk was when he stepped in the cow pat!
The word is **humorous**.

Spelling 12: The word is **exception**.
The teacher made an **exception** and let the children play on the grass.
The word is **exception**.

Spelling 13: The word is **confession**.
The burglar's **confession** helped them to find the missing jewels.
The word is **confession**.

Spelling 14: The word is **intention**.
It is my **intention** to finish school early.
The word is **intention**.

Spelling 15: The word is **beautician**.
The **beautician** painted the lady's nails purple.
The word is **beautician**.

Spelling 16: The word is **operation**.
She needed an **operation** on her broken arm.
The word is **operation**.

Spelling 17: The word is **situation**.
The police officer calmed down the **situation**.
The word is **situation**.

Spelling 18: The word is **decision**.
The umpire's **decision** was final.
The word is **decision**.

Spelling 19: The word is **illusion**.
The game gave the **illusion** that you were in a rainforest.
The word is **illusion**.

Spelling 20: The word is **optician**.
The **optician** said I needed glasses.
The word is **optician**.

Well done! Now I will read the sentences again so you can check your spelling.

| Name | Class | Date |

Year 4/P5 Summer Half Term 1 Test A

1. The _____ dog swam to the sinking boat.

2. The dance _____ was hard to copy.

3. _____ to the museum took ages.

4. At school we do reading _____ tests.

5. The _____ waved his wand and disappeared.

6. The _____ model strutted down the catwalk.

7. Hybrid cars are a modern _____.

8. The _____ failed because everyone spoke at once.

9. The _____ lead was stretched as Dad tried to reach the fence with his drill.

10. The _____ set up his guitar and amp.

11. The most _____ moment of the walk was when he stepped in the cow pat!

12. The teacher made an _____ and let the children play on the grass.

13. The burglar's _____ helped them to find the missing jewels.

14. It is my _____ to finish school early.

15. The _____ painted the lady's nails purple.

16. She needed an _____ on her broken arm.

17. The police officer calmed down the _____.

18. The umpire's _____ was final.

19. The game gave the _____ that you were in a rainforest.

20. The _____ said I needed glasses.

Total _____ / 20

Year 4/P5 Summer Half Term 1 Test B

Spelling rules and knowledge

- The suffix **-ous**
- Endings spelt **-tion**, **-tian**, **-sion**, **-cian**, **-ssion**

Guidance for teachers

The test is designed to build experience and confidence with this format, as well as to test children's spelling knowledge.
The test should take approximately 15 minutes.
Children should have a copy of the test and a pencil to use.
Children with specific needs should be given appropriate support.
All children should be encouraged to have a go at spelling each word, using the strategies that they have learnt.
Remind the children to check their answers by asking: *Does it look right? Does it sound right?*
Avoid over-emphasising the spelling of each word as you read it.

> Read each word aloud, saying: *The word is…*
> Next, read the sentence that includes the word.
> Wait for the children to attempt to write the word.
> Re-read the word, saying: *The word is…*

Remind the children to check the word before moving to the next spelling.
At the end of the test, read each sentence again and encourage the children to check back.

Instructions for children

(You may like to read this to the children prior to the test.)

This is a spelling test to check your knowledge of the spelling patterns we have worked on this half term.
You need a pencil.
Please write your name, class and the date at the top of the test.
I will read a word out loud and then say it again in a sentence.
You should write the word in the gap in the sentence on your test.
I will read it again and give you time to check it.
Don't worry if you are not sure about a spelling. Have a go using the strategies we have learnt.
If you make a mistake, cross out the word and try again.

Words tested (20)

vigorous, injection, expression, expansion, electrician, outrageous, hesitation, permission, attention, mathematician, rigorous, completion, persuasion, tension, politician, relation, imagination, suspicion, conclusion, technician

Year 4/P5 Summer Half Term 1 Test B

Spelling script

Spelling 1: The word is **vigorous**.
Vigorous exercise makes you sweaty.
The word is **vigorous**.

Spelling 2: The word is **injection**.
The nurse had to give him an **injection**.
The word is **injection**.

Spelling 3: The word is **expression**.
The **expression** on her face showed that she was nervous.
The word is **expression**.

Spelling 4: The word is **expansion**.
The playground's **expansion** was helped by the money raised at the summer fair.
The word is **expansion**.

Spelling 5: The word is **electrician**.
The **electrician** found the fault in the wiring.
The word is **electrician**.

Spelling 6: The word is **outrageous**.
The clown's antics were **outrageous**.
The word is **outrageous**.

Spelling 7: The word is **hesitation**.
Without **hesitation**, the boy helped the elderly man to cross the road.
The word is **hesitation**.

Spelling 8: The word is **permission**.
She was given **permission** to go on the holiday.
The word is **permission**.

Spelling 9: The word is **attention**.
It is hard to pay **attention** when you are hungry.
The word is **attention**.

Spelling 10: The word is **mathematician**.
The **mathematician** loved to solve puzzles.
The word is **mathematician**.

Spelling 11: The word is **rigorous**.
The trial for the football academy was **rigorous**.
The word is **rigorous**.

Spelling 12: The word is **completion**.
Completion of the puzzle filled me with satisfaction.
The word is **completion**.

Spelling 13: The word is **persuasion**.
I am open to **persuasion** about going to the beach!
The word is **persuasion**.

Spelling 14: The word is **tension**.
We felt the **tension** before our dance exam!
The word is **tension**.

Spelling 15: The word is **politician**.
The **politician** hoped people would vote for her.
The word is **politician**.

Spelling 16: The word is **relation**.
My grandad is my favourite **relation**.
The word is **relation**.

Spelling 17: The word is **imagination**.
When we write a story, we have to use our **imagination**.
The word is **imagination**.

Spelling 18: The word is **suspicion**.
She had a **suspicion** that he was telling a lie.
The word is **suspicion**.

Spelling 19: The word is **conclusion**.
The **conclusion** of the story was so exciting!
The word is **conclusion**.

Spelling 20: The word is **technician**.
The ski **technician** waxed my skis to make them slide.
The word is **technician**.

Well done! Now I will read the sentences again so you can check your spelling.

| Name | Class | Date |

Year 4/P5 Summer Half Term 1 Test B

1. _____ exercise makes you sweaty.

2. The nurse had to give him an _____.

3. The _____ on her face showed that she was nervous.

4. The playground's _____ was helped by the money raised at the summer fair.

5. The _____ found the fault in the wiring.

6. The clown's antics were _____.

7. Without _____, the boy helped the elderly man to cross the road.

8. She was given _____ to go on the holiday.

9. It is hard to pay _____ when you are hungry.

10. The _____ loved to solve puzzles.

11. The trial for the football academy was _____.

12. _____ of the puzzle filled me with satisfaction.

13. I am open to _____ about going to the beach!

14. We felt the _____ before our dance exam!

15. The _____ hoped people would vote for her.

16. My grandad is my favourite _____.

17. When we write a story, we have to use our _____.

18. She had a _____ that he was telling a lie.

19. The _____ of the story was so exciting!

20. The ski _____ waxed my skis to make them slide.

Total _____ / 20

Year 4/P5 Summer Half Term 2 Test A

Spelling rules and knowledge

- The sound made by **ch** in words like *scheme, chorus*
- The sound made by **ch** in words like *chef, chalet*
- The sound made by **-gue** and **-que** at the end of words
- The sound made by **sc** in words like *scene*
- The sound made by **ei** in words like *vein*
- Word list – Years 3 and 4

Guidance for teachers

The test is designed to build experience and confidence with this format, as well as to test children's spelling knowledge.
The test should take approximately 15 minutes.
Children should have a copy of the test and a pencil to use.
Children with specific needs should be given appropriate support.
All children should be encouraged to have a go at spelling each word, using the strategies that they have learnt.
Remind the children to check their answers by asking: *Does it look right? Does it sound right?*
Avoid over-emphasising the spelling of each word as you read it.

> Read each word aloud, saying: *The word is…*
> Next, read the sentence that includes the word.
> Wait for the children to attempt to write the word.
> Re-read the word, saying: *The word is…*

Remind the children to check the word before moving to the next spelling.
At the end of the test, read each sentence again and encourage the children to check back.

Instructions for children

(You may like to read this to the children prior to the test.)

This is a spelling test to check your knowledge of the spelling patterns we have worked on this half term.
You need a pencil.
Please write your name, class and the date at the top of the test.
I will read a word out loud and then say it again in a sentence.
You should write the word in the gap in the sentence on your test.
I will read it again and give you time to check it.
Don't worry if you are not sure about a spelling. Have a go using the strategies we have learnt.
If you make a mistake, cross out the word and try again.

Words tested (20)

machine, mosque, crescent, prey, actually, chorus, tongue, science, neighbour, accident, chemist, dialogue, discipline, grey, address, chef, vague, scent, weigh, bicycle

Year 4/P5 Summer Half Term 2 Test A

Spelling script

Spelling 1: The word is **machine**.
The washing **machine** spun out of control.
The word is **machine**.

Spelling 2: The word is **mosque**.
The **mosque** is a place of learning and prayer.
The word is **mosque**.

Spelling 3: The word is **crescent**.
The **crescent** moon glimmered in the night sky.
The word is **crescent**.

Spelling 4: The word is **prey**.
The lion's **prey** ran for cover.
The word is **prey**.

Spelling 5: The word is **actually**.
Actually, I can ride a bike without using my hands!
The word is **actually**.

Spelling 6: The word is **chorus**.
We can join in with the song's **chorus**.
The word is **chorus**.

Spelling 7: The word is **tongue**.
Ouch! I have an ulcer under my **tongue**.
The word is **tongue**.

Spelling 8: The word is **science**.
In **science** we learn about the human body.
The word is **science**.

Spelling 9: The word is **neighbour**.
My **neighbour** lets us play in her back garden.
The word is **neighbour**.

Spelling 10: The word is **accident**.
The **accident** left the bike with a crumpled wheel.
The word is **accident**.

Spelling 11: The word is **chemist**.
The **chemist** told me to take some painkillers.
The word is **chemist**.

Spelling 12: **dialogue**.
We had to read the **dialogue** in the playscript.
The word is **dialogue**.

Spelling 13: The word is **discipline**.
In the army, the **discipline** is very strict.
The word is **discipline**.

Spelling 14: The word is **grey**.
The old **grey** donkey loved to eat apples.
The word is **grey**.

Spelling 15: The word is **address**.
When we moved, our **address** changed.
The word is **address**.

Spelling 16: The word is **chef**.
The **chef** prepared a sumptuous banquet.
The word is **chef**.

Spelling 17: The word is **vague**.
My memories about starting school are **vague**.
The word is **vague**.

Spelling 18: The word is **scent**.
The police dog followed the burglar's **scent**.
The word is **scent**.

Spelling 19: The word is **weigh**.
Please **weigh** out the ingredients for the cake.
The word is **weigh**.

Spelling 20: The word is **bicycle**.
She whizzed down the hill on her **bicycle**.
The word is **bicycle**.

Well done! Now I will read the sentences again so you can check your spelling.

| Name | Class | Date |

Year 4/P5 Summer Half Term 2 Test A

1. The washing _____ spun out of control.

2. The _____ is a place of learning and prayer.

3. The _____ moon glimmered in the night sky.

4. The lion's _____ ran for cover.

5. _____, I can ride a bike without using my hands!

6. We can join in with the song's _____.

7. Ouch! I have an ulcer under my _____.

8. In _____ we learn about the human body.

9. My _____ lets us play in her back garden.

10. The _____ left the bike with a crumpled wheel.

11. The _____ told me to take some painkillers.

12. We had to read the _____ in the playscript.

13. In the army, the _____ is very strict.

14. The old _____ donkey loved to eat apples.

15. When we moved, our _____ changed.

16. The _____ prepared a sumptuous banquet.

17. My memories about starting school are _____.

18. The police dog followed the burglar's _____.

19. Please _____ out the ingredients for the cake.

20. She whizzed down the hill on her _____.

Total _____ / 20

Year 4/P5 Summer Half Term 2 Test B

Spelling rules and knowledge

- The sound made by **ch** in words like *scheme, chorus*
- The sound made by **ch** in words like *chef, chalet*
- The sound made by **-gue** and **-que** at the end of words
- The sound made by **sc** in words like *scene*
- The sound made by **ei** in words like *vein*
- Word list – Years 3 and 4

Guidance for teachers

The test is designed to build experience and confidence with this format, as well as to test children's spelling knowledge.
The test should take approximately 15 minutes.
Children should have a copy of the test and a pencil to use.
Children with specific needs should be given appropriate support.
All children should be encouraged to have a go at spelling each word, using the strategies that they have learnt.
Remind the children to check their answers by asking: *Does it look right? Does it sound right?*
Avoid over-emphasising the spelling of each word as you read it.

> Read each word aloud, saying: *The word is…*
> Next, read the sentence that includes the word.
> Wait for the children to attempt to write the word.
> Re-read the word, saying: *The word is…*

Remind the children to check the word before moving to the next spelling.
At the end of the test, read each sentence again and encourage the children to check back.

Instructions for children

(You may like to read this to the children prior to the test.)

This is a spelling test to check your knowledge of the spelling patterns we have worked on this half term.
You need a pencil.
Please write your name, class and the date at the top of the test.
I will read a word out loud and then say it again in a sentence.
You should write the word in the gap in the sentence on your test.
I will read it again and give you time to check it.
Don't worry if you are not sure about a spelling. Have a go using the strategies we have learnt.
If you make a mistake, cross out the word and try again.

Words tested (20)

character, catalogue, scissors, reign, believe, chalet, unique, muscle, obey, appear, scheme, antique, scenery, they, arrive, echo, league, fascinate, vein, answer

Year 4/P5 Summer Half Term 2 Test B

Spelling script

Spelling 1: The word is **character**.
The evil **character** in the play was super scary.
The word is **character**.

Spelling 2: The word is **catalogue**.
We looked in the **catalogue** for new toys.
The word is **catalogue**.

Spelling 3: The word is **scissors**.
I cut my finger on the sharp **scissors**.
The word is **scissors**.

Spelling 4: The word is **reign**.
Queen Victoria's **reign** lasted for over 60 years.
The word is **reign**.

Spelling 5: The word is **believe**.
Do you **believe** that there is gold at the end of the rainbow?
The word is **believe**.

Spelling 6: The word is **chalet**.
The fire roared in the cosy ski **chalet**.
The word is **chalet**.

Spelling 7: The word is **unique**.
Every fingerprint is **unique**.
The word is **unique**.

Spelling 8: The word is **muscle**.
She pulled a **muscle** at netball training.
The word is **muscle**.

Spelling 9: The word is **obey**.
We **obey** the rules, so that the game can be played.
The word is **obey**.

Spelling 10: The word is **appear**.
The children didn't **appear** when they were called for their lunch.
The word is **appear**.

Spelling 11: The word is **scheme**.
The reading **scheme** was divided into colours.
The word is **scheme**.

Spelling 12: The word is **antique**.
The **antique** shop was like Aladdin's cave!
The word is **antique**.

Spelling 13: The word is **scenery**.
The mountain **scenery** was spectacular.
The word is **scenery**.

Spelling 14: The word is **they**.
They rushed to the door when the bell rang.
The word is **they**.

Spelling 15: The word is **arrive**.
We hope that the sun will shine when we **arrive** at the beach.
The word is **arrive**.

Spelling 16: The word is **echo**.
We heard an **echo** of our voices in the cave.
The word is **echo**.

Spelling 17: The word is **league**.
We came top of the **league**!
The word is **league**.

Spelling 18: The word is **fascinate**.
We **fascinate** our kitten with a fishing toy.
The word is **fascinate**.

Spelling 19: The word is **vein**.
The **vein** in my leg carries blood back to my heart.
The word is **vein**.

Spelling 20: The word is **answer**.
It is polite to **answer** when people ask you a question.
The word is **answer**.

Well done! Now I will read the sentences again so you can check your spelling.

| Name | Class | Date |

Year 4/P5 Summer Half Term 2 Test B

1. The evil _____ in the play was super scary.

2. We looked in the _____ for new toys.

3. I cut my finger on the sharp _____.

4. Queen Victoria's _____ lasted for over 60 years.

5. Do you _____ that there is gold at the end of the rainbow?

6. The fire roared in the cosy ski _____.

7. Every fingerprint is _____.

8. She pulled a _____ at netball training.

9. We _____ the rules, so that the game can be played.

10. The children didn't _____ when they were called for their lunch.

11. The reading _____ was divided into colours.

12. The _____ shop was like Aladdin's cave!

13. The mountain _____ was spectacular.

14. _____ rushed to the door when the bell rang.

15. We hope that the sun will shine when we _____ at the beach.

16. We heard an _____ of our voices in the cave.

17. We came top of the _____!

18. We _____ our kitten with a fishing toy.

19. The _____ in my leg carries blood back to my heart.

20. It is polite to _____ when people ask you a question.

Total _____ / 20

Answers in Context

Year 4/P5 Autumn Half Term 1 Test A

1. Stand in a **circle** and hold hands.

2. The spellings became more **difficult** as the children got older.

3. In England in **February**, it is likely to be cold.

4. Close your eyes and **imagine** you are relaxing on a sandy beach.

5. We have to **learn** our times tables.

6. We love to **build** sand sculptures.

7. Please **continue** to read the book in silence.

8. When you have eaten **enough** pasta, please clear the table.

9. The **guard** dog snarled and bared its teeth.

10. She carried the **important** message to the office.

Answers in Context

11. I am **certain** that I asked you to brush your hair!

12. We like to be **early** for the bus.

13. The scientist's **experiment** went drastically wrong.

14. The **height** of the tower made me feel giddy.

15. His **knowledge** of international football players was extraordinary.

16. Please add the girls' birthdays to the **calendar**.

17. Spiders usually have **eight** legs.

18. The world-**famous** opera singer bowed to the applause.

19. We can learn about our local **history** by looking at the local buildings.

20. We visit the **library** to borrow interesting books.

Answers in Context

Year 4/P5 Autumn Half Term 1 Test B

1. How many years are there in a **century**?

2. The **earth** spins on its own axis every day.

3. We **exercise** to keep our hearts strong and healthy.

4. Pineapple is a delicious yellow **fruit**.

5. The pirates landed on Treasure **Island**.

6. We **breathe** air into our lungs.

7. Please don't **disappear** when I need you!

8. Cola is my **favourite** fizzy drink.

9. How many times does your **heart** beat each minute?

10. We had to sort each different **material** in science.

Answers in Context

11. He told us to mind our own **business**!

12. I can't **decide** between cake and ice cream.

13. Riding the zip-wire was a thrilling **experience**.

14. The **guide** led us around the ruined temple.

15. The boy's **interest** in birdwatching was obvious.

16. Stand in the **centre** of the circle and spin three times.

17. Please **consider** what you would like to do when you grow up.

18. The **extreme** conditions meant we couldn't climb the mountain.

19. The **group** of monkeys raced after the bananas.

20. I would love my pocket money to **increase**!

Answers in Context

Year 4/P5 Autumn Half Term 2 Test A

1. Today was no **ordinary** day!

2. **Perhaps** you would like to see a film tonight?

3. Can you **remember** learning to write your name?

4. **Although** he was tired, he managed to stay awake for the party.

5. Let's make ourselves **busy** so we don't feel bored.

6. The **naughty** monkey loved to play tricks.

7. Spinning around can give you a **peculiar** sensation.

8. Some children start school at **quarter** to nine.

9. Can you **separate** the egg yolk from the white?

10. He **thought** really hard before choosing his gift.

Answers in Context

11. The wedding was a joyful **occasion**.

12. Which **position** would you like to play in today?

13. I always order a **regular** sized drink.

14. The **strange** smell wafted through the room.

15. Some **women** drove army vehicles during the Second World War.

16. In a **minute**, we will be able to go out to play.

17. Rabbits are **popular** pets for children.

18. He forgot his PE bag on **purpose**.

19. I **suppose** you would like to share my sweets?

20. She took a deep **breath** before diving in.

Answers in Context

Year 4/P5 Autumn Half Term 2 Test B

1. She was a **natural** swimmer.

2. We mash **potatoes** with butter and cream.

3. She will **probably** arrive early.

4. He liked to drink his tea from a **special** cup.

5. They wriggled **through** the gap in the fence and into the woods.

6. What is the **opposite** of hot?

7. Would it be **possible** for my child to stand in front of you?

8. I am sure you can answer this **question**.

9. The beautiful flowers were a lovely **surprise** for Mum.

10. We shared the sweets into two **equal** piles.

Answers in Context

11. The police officer didn't **notice** the car as it jumped the red light.

12. We don't **possess** enough information to decide who should win.

13. The most **recent** addition to their collection of pets was a baby hamster.

14. Even **though** the water was chilly, we dived in.

15. The super-fit elderly **woman** cycled up the hill and overtook the young cyclist.

16. Please don't **mention** the spot on my nose!

17. She was **particular** about what she would eat.

18. I said I would never break a **promise**.

19. Roman roads were usually long and **straight**.

20. The plants were grown in pots of **various** sizes.

Answers in Context

Year 4/P5 Spring Half Term 1 Test A

1. We tried not to **disappoint** our teacher!

2. The old man was slightly deaf so he **misheard** the children.

3. The coach became **impatient** as he waited for his players to change.

4. You need to **refresh** the browser to make the search engine work.

5. We hate shopping in the **supermarket**.

6. The prisoner didn't dare to **disobey** the guard.

7. The children tried not to **misbehave** in class.

8. It is **illegal** to ride a bicycle on a motorway.

9. I need to **return** the faulty television to the shop.

10. Life on a **submarine** is very cramped!

Answers in Context

11. He loved to **disappear** just before bedtime!

12. Don't **misjudge** a book before reading it.

13. The little boy seemed **immature** to his older brother.

14. We must **reapply** the paint where it has peeled.

15. We tried to **submerge** an inflated rubber ring.

16. The shopkeeper's **distrust** was obvious when he saw the children enter the shop.

17. The teacher smiled even though the child's answer was **incorrect**.

18. Who won the match was **irrelevant** to the proud coach.

19. The girl was desperate to **repaint** her bedroom.

20. Fold the paper in half, then **subdivide** it again.

Answers in Context

Year 4/P5 Spring Half Term 1 Test B

1. Would anyone like to **disagree** with the argument?

2. News reports can **mislead** you.

3. The china cup was **imperfect** and had to be returned to the shop.

4. Can you **replay** the video and watch it again?

5. The **subtotal** on the bill was £35.00.

6. Many children **dislike** aubergines.

7. Research proves that it is unhealthy to be **inactive** for too long each day.

8. It was **impossible** to stop the snowman from melting.

9. Why don't you **rearrange** your bedroom?

10. Every talent show has a **superstar**.

Answers in Context

11. No-one trusted the **dishonest** cyclist.

12. It is easy to **misspell** words with prefixes!

13. The old man's hand shook so his handwriting was **illegible**.

14. She had to **retake** the selfie.

15. In a book, a **subtitle** can give the reader more information about the content.

16. The rider struggled to **dismount** from her horse.

17. They had the **misfortune** to lose their tortoise.

18. The **irresponsible** boy forgot his homework.

19. We can **redecorate** in any colour we want!

20. We use the **subway** to reach the other side of the busy road safely.

Answers in Context

Year 4/P5 Spring Half Term 2 Test A

1. The magical clock's hands moved in an **anticlockwise** direction.

2. The children loved to explore the **nature** around them.

3. Aeroplane pilots need perfect **vision**.

4. The busy road was known for being **dangerous**.

5. She was **jealous** of her friend's pierced ears.

6. We took the **intercity** train to Glasgow.

7. Please **measure** the hall with a metre stick.

8. The teacher's **decision** was final.

9. The **poisonous** viper had beautiful markings.

10. The **enormous** garden gnome toppled into the pond with a splash.

Answers in Context

11. Sports people often write their **autobiography**.

12. The glimmering scaly **creature** emerged from beneath the waves.

13. I would love a **television** in my bedroom!

14. Jumping into the freezing river was a **spontaneous** action.

15. The children gave a **tremendous** cheer as their head teacher finished the race.

16. The **international** airport was always busy.

17. I dream of finding **treasure** on a faraway island.

18. The girls had to do **revision** at the weekend.

19. The **courteous** boy held the door open for us.

20. The **hideous** weather stopped us from going camping at half term.

Answers in Context

Year 4/P5 Spring Half Term 2 Test B

1. Mum used **antiseptic** on my grazed knee.

2. It was a **pleasure** to see my cousins.

3. The **collision** left the driver shaken.

4. Wales is a **mountainous** country.

5. The solution to the problem was **obvious**.

6. I asked the pop star for her **autograph**.

7. He took a **picture** with his mobile phone.

8. Shortly after the **explosion**, the fire engine arrived.

9. We want to see the **famous** singer.

10. The chocolate cake was absolutely **delicious**.

Answers in Context

11. Can you **intertwine** your fingers?

12. We moved the **furniture** to look for the gerbil.

13. She caused **confusion** by arriving a day early for the meeting.

14. We were **cautious** when we held the tarantula.

15. The **serious** gentleman's face broke into a smile.

16. He felt **antisocial** so he didn't go to the party.

17. We can do trampolining at the **leisure** centre.

18. **Division** problems can be trickier than multiplication problems.

19. The **curious** cat peered at its reflection in the pond.

20. We tried **various** methods to solve the problem.

© HarperCollins Publishers Ltd 2018

Answers in Context

Year 4/P5 Summer Half Term 1 Test A

1. The **courageous** dog swam to the sinking boat.

2. The dance **action** was hard to copy.

3. **Admission** to the museum took ages.

4. At school we do reading **comprehension** tests.

5. The **magician** waved his wand and disappeared.

6. The **glamorous** model strutted down the catwalk.

7. Hybrid cars are a modern **invention**.

8. The **discussion** failed because everyone spoke at once.

9. The **extension** lead was stretched as Dad tried to reach the fence with his drill.

10. The **musician** set up his guitar and amp.

Answers in Context

11. The most **humorous** moment of the walk was when he stepped in the cow pat!

12. The teacher made an **exception** and let the children play on the grass.

13. The burglar's **confession** helped them to find the missing jewels.

14. It is my **intention** to finish school early.

15. The **beautician** painted the lady's nails purple.

16. She needed an **operation** on her broken arm.

17. The police officer calmed down the **situation**.

18. The umpire's **decision** was final.

19. The game gave the **illusion** that you were in a rainforest.

20. The **optician** said I needed glasses.

Answers in Context

Year 4/P5 Summer Half Term 1 Test B

1. **Vigorous** exercise makes you sweaty.

2. The nurse had to give him an **injection**.

3. The **expression** on her face showed that she was nervous.

4. The playground's **expansion** was helped by the money raised at the summer fair.

5. The **electrician** found the fault in the wiring.

6. The clown's antics were **outrageous**.

7. Without **hesitation**, the boy helped the elderly man to cross the road.

8. She was given **permission** to go on the holiday.

9. It is hard to pay **attention** when you are hungry.

10. The **mathematician** loved to solve puzzles.

Answers in Context

11. The trial for the football academy was **rigorous**.

12. **Completion** of the puzzle filled me with satisfaction.

13. I am open to **persuasion** about going to the beach!

14. We felt the **tension** before our dance exam!

15. The **politician** hoped people would vote for her.

16. My grandad is my favourite **relation**.

17. When we write a story, we have to use our **imagination**.

18. She had a **suspicion** that he was telling a lie.

19. The **conclusion** of the story was so exciting!

20. The ski **technician** waxed my skis to make them slide.

Answers in Context

Year 4/P5 Summer Half Term 2 Test A

1. The washing **machine** spun out of control.

2. The **mosque** is a place of learning and prayer.

3. The **crescent** moon glimmered in the night sky.

4. The lion's **prey** ran for cover.

5. **Actually**, I can ride a bike without using my hands!

6. We can join in with the song's **chorus**.

7. Ouch! I have an ulcer under my **tongue**.

8. In **science** we learn about the human body.

9. My **neighbour** lets us play in her back garden.

10. The **accident** left the bike with a crumpled wheel.

Answers in Context

11. The **chemist** told me to take some painkillers.

12. We had to read the **dialogue** in the playscript.

13. In the army, the **discipline** is very strict.

14. The old **grey** donkey loved to eat apples.

15. When we moved, our **address** changed.

16. The **chef** prepared a sumptuous banquet.

17. My memories about starting school are **vague**.

18. The police dog followed the burglar's **scent**.

19. Please **weigh** out the ingredients for the cake.

20. She whizzed down the hill on her **bicycle**.

Answers in Context

Year 4/P5 Summer Half Term 2 Test B

1. The evil **character** in the play was super scary.

2. We looked in the **catalogue** for new toys.

3. I cut my finger on the sharp **scissors**.

4. Queen Victoria's **reign** lasted for over 60 years.

5. Do you **believe** that there is gold at the end of the rainbow?

6. The fire roared in the cosy ski **chalet**.

7. Every fingerprint is **unique**.

8. She pulled a **muscle** at netball training.

9. We **obey** the rules, so that the game can be played.

10. The children didn't **appear** when they were called for their lunch.

Answers in Context

11. The reading **scheme** was divided into colours.

12. The **antique** shop was like Aladdin's cave!

13. The mountain **scenery** was spectacular.

14. **They** rushed to the door when the bell rang.

15. We hope that the sun will shine when we **arrive** at the beach.

16. We heard an **echo** of our voices in the cave.

17. We came top of the **league**!

18. We **fascinate** our kitten with a fishing toy.

19. The **vein** in my leg carries blood back to my heart.

20. It is polite to **answer** when people ask you a question.

Word-only Answers

Year 4/P5 Autumn Half Term 1 Test A
1. circle, 2. difficult, 3. February, 4. imagine,
5. learn, 6. build, 7. continue, 8. enough,
9. guard, 10. important, 11. certain, 12. early,
13. experiment, 14. height, 15. knowledge,
16. calendar, 17. eight, 18. famous, 19. history,
20. library

Year 4/P5 Autumn Half Term 1 Test B
1. century, 2. earth, 3. exercise, 4. fruit, 5. island, 6. breathe, 7. disappear, 8. favourite, 9. heart, 10. material, 11. business, 12. decide,
13. experience, 14. guide, 15. interest,
16. centre, 17. consider, 18. extreme, 19. group, 20. increase

Year 4/P5 Autumn Half Term 2 Test A
1. ordinary, 2. perhaps, 3. remember,
4. although, 5. busy, 6. naughty, 7. peculiar,
8. quarter, 9. separate, 10. thought,
11. occasion, 12. position, 13. regular,
14. strange, 15. women, 16. minute, 17. popular, 18. purpose, 19. suppose, 20. breath

Year 4/P5 Autumn Half Term 2 Test B
1. natural, 2. potatoes, 3. probably, 4. special,
5. through, 6. opposite, 7. possible, 8. question,
9. surprise, 10. equal, 11. notice, 12. possess,
13. recent, 14. though, 15. woman, 16. mention,
17. particular, 18. promise, 19. straight,
20. various

Year 4/P5 Spring Half Term 1 Test A
1. disappoint, 2. misheard, 3. impatient,
4. refresh, 5. supermarket, 6. disobey,
7. misbehave, 8. illegal, 9. return, 10. submarine, 11. disappear, 12. misjudge, 13. immature,
14. reapply, 15. submerge, 16. distrust,
17. incorrect, 18. irrelevant, 19. repaint,
20. subdivide

Year 4/P5 Spring Half Term 1 Test B
1. disagree, 2. mislead, 3. imperfect, 4. replay,
5. subtotal, 6. dislike, 7. inactive, 8. impossible,
9. rearrange, 10. superstar, 11. dishonest,
12. misspell, 13. illegible, 14. retake, 15. subtitle, 16. dismount, 17. misfortune, 18. irresponsible, 19. redecorate, 20. subway

Year 4/P5 Spring Half Term 2 Test A
1. anticlockwise, 2. nature, 3. vision,
4. dangerous, 5. jealous, 6. intercity, 7. measure, 8. decision, 9. poisonous, 10. enormous,
11. autobiography, 12. creature, 13. television,
14. spontaneous, 15. tremendous,
16. international, 17. treasure, 18. revision,
19. courteous, 20. hideous

Year 4/P5 Spring Half Term 2 Test B
1. antiseptic, 2. pleasure, 3. collision,
4. mountainous, 5. obvious, 6. autograph,
7. picture, 8. explosion, 9. famous, 10. delicious, 11. intertwine, 12. furniture, 13. confusion,
14. cautious, 15. serious, 16. antisocial,
17. leisure, 18. division, 19. curious, 20. various

Word-only Answers

Year 4/P5 Summer Half Term 1 Test A
1. courageous, 2. action, 3. admission,
4. comprehension, 5. magician, 6. glamorous,
7. invention, 8. discussion, 9. extension,
10. musician, 11. humorous, 12. exception,
13. confession, 14. intention, 15. beautician,
16. operation, 17. situation, 18. decision,
19. illusion, 20. optician

Year 4/P5 Summer Half Term 1 Test B
1. vigorous, 2. injection, 3. expression,
4. expansion, 5. electrician, 6. outrageous,
7. hesitation, 8. permission, 9. attention,
10. mathematician, 11. rigorous, 12. completion, 13. persuasion, 14. tension, 15. politician,
16. relation, 17. imagination, 18. suspicion,
19. conclusion, 20. technician

Year 4/P5 Summer Half Term 2 Test A
1. machine, 2. mosque, 3. crescent, 4. prey,
5. actually, 6. chorus, 7. tongue, 8. science,
9. neighbour, 10. accident, 11. chemist,
12. dialogue, 13. discipline, 14. grey,
15. address, 16. chef, 17. vague, 18. scent,
19. weigh, 20. bicycle

Year 4/P5 Summer Half Term 2 Test B
1. character, 2. catalogue, 3. scissors, 4. reign,
5. believe, 6. chalet, 7. unique, 8. muscle,
9. obey, 10. appear, 11. scheme, 12. antique,
13. scenery, 14. they, 15. arrive, 16. echo,
17. league, 18. fascinate, 19. vein, 20. answer

Name	Class

Year 4/P5 Spelling Record Sheet

Tests	Mark	Total marks	Key words to target
Autumn Half Term 1 Test A		20	
Autumn Half Term 1 Test B		20	
Autumn Half Term 2 Test A		20	
Autumn Half Term 2 Test B		20	
Spring Half Term 1 Test A		20	
Spring Half Term 1 Test B		20	
Spring Half Term 2 Test A		20	
Spring Half Term 2 Test B		20	
Summer Half Term 1 Test A		20	
Summer Half Term 1 Test B		20	
Summer Half Term 2 Test A		20	
Summer Half Term 2 Test B		20	

© HarperCollins*Publishers* Ltd 2018